Backpack

SURVIVAL GUIDE

Brought to you by the
WILDERNESS SCHOOL
INSTITUTE

Copyright © 2019 Wilderness School Institute

All rights reserved.

ISBN: 978-1-944798-29-1

No part of this book may be reproduced or transmitted in any form or by any means electronic or mechanical, including photocopying, recording, or by any information storage and retrieval system, without the written permission of the publisher.

Published in the United States by:

Summers Island Press
P.O. Box 19293
Thorne Bay, Alaska 99919

Website: www.SummersIslandPress.com

For information contact:
info@summersislandpress.com

Summers Island Press is an imprint of the Wilderness School Institute, a non-profit educational organization that offers outdoor youth activities in wilderness settings, including training in wilderness skills and nature studies, as well as the publication of curriculum on related subjects, through their book imprints Summers Island Press and Lightsmith Publishers.

Summers Island Press
Thorne Bay, Alaska

To all those who would like to know how to take care of themselves and others when they are out and about in the wilderness.

A Word From The Wilderness Expert

Hello Adventurers!

Thank you for picking up this great booklet on outdoor skills. I wanted to make sure you all understood the most important thing about being in the wilderness. When you are in the city there are lots of signs keeping you safe. There are different signs in the woods. In the wilderness, you need to be watching for these signs all the time. That is why your brain is your most important asset in the woods. Practice using your brain, increase your powers of observation at home, and it will serve you well when you are in the woods.

The Wilderness Expert.

CONTENTS

10 Things You Need to Survive

What the Army Says

Building A Fire

Making a Shelter

What To Do If You Are Lost

Finding Your Way

Some Good Things To Know

A Prayer If You Are In Serious Trouble

A Word From the Wilderness Expert

The Wilderness Expert says:

You should always have these ten things on hand, in a backpack or go-bag, even if you are only out on a day hike. Because you never know when an emergency might come along and you will have to deal with it whether you're ready, or not.

Then you will be ready for any situation, whatever that happens to be.

10 Things You Need to SURVIVE

◄─────────────────────►

NAVIGATION
(map and compass)

SUN PROTECTION
(sunglasses and sunscreen)

INSULATION
(extra clothing)

ILLUMINATION
(flashlight/headlamp)

FIRST AID KIT

FIRE STARTER
(waterproof matches, flint, lighter, etc.)

NUTRITION AND HYDRATION
(extra food and water)

KNIFE (or multi-tool)

EMERGENCY SHELTER
(poncho, tarp, sleeping bag, etc.)

COMMUNICATION
(Whistle, signaling mirror, notepad, etc)

The Wilderness Expert says:

■■■➤

The best part of this is **V—Vanquish fear!** The word vanquish is just a super strong way to say destroy fear like an enemy. How do you do that? Stop what you are doing, focus on something like breathing, and say "I vanquish fear!" until you feel better. It works.

The Army says:

- **S** Size up the situation.
- **U** Use all your senses.
- **R** Remember where you are.
- ┅➡ **V** **Vanquish fear and panic.**
- **I** Improvise.
- **V** Value living,
- **A** Act like the natives.
- **L** Live by your wits.
  (but for now, learn basic skills).

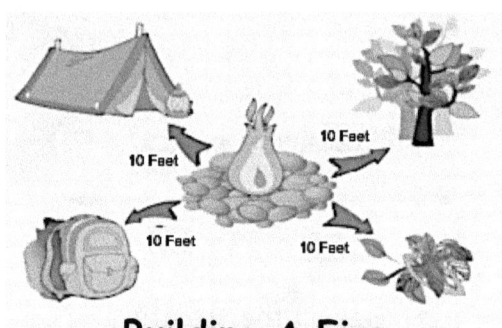

Building A Fire

*Two things are essential in the building of a fire —**kindling** and **air**. A fire must be built systematically.*

First, get some dry, small, dead branches, twigs, and other flammable material. Place these on the ground. Be sure air will be able to get under it and up through it. Start with a few bits and splinters of dry wood (tinder), two or three small dry sticks, and light them on fire.

*"**If you have no matches**, you can strike a spark with a flint and steel (the back of your knife on a stone will do it), and so start a bit of dry grass or moss smoking which you can then blow gently into flame. Or, you can do it with a magnifying glass if there is a good sun shining, by making the sunlight pass through*

the glass onto a small amount of tinder." (Sir Robert Baden-Powell)

Next, add heavier sticks until you have built the camp fire as large as you need it. The great art is to begin with a very small fire and a very dry one. You can then add to its size, later on. When it is going strong, you can add damper wood, if dry wood is scarce. Birch-bark cannot be found everywhere, but it is the best of tinder when you have it.

Never build a large camp fire too near the tent or flammable pine trees. Better build it in the open. Be careful to prevent the spreading of fire. This may be done by building a circle of stones around the fire, or by digging up the earth, or by wetting a space around the fire. Try to have buckets of water near at hand.

To prevent the re-kindling of fire after it is

apparently out, pour water over it and soak the earth for two or three feet around it. This is very important, for many forest fires have started through failure to do this. Things to remember: It is criminal to leave a burning fire; always put it out with water or dirt. A fire is never out until the last spark is extinguished. Sometimes a log will smolder after the flames look like they're gone only to break out, again, with a rising wind.

FIRE READY FOR LIGHTING.

Begin in a small way by putting first some dry "kindling" or small splinters and shavings, dry grass, or a *little* paper, anything that will easily take fire, and over that stack a lot of small dry sticks, standing on end and leaning together, or leaning against a log – on the *windward* side of it. Remember, dry *sticks* are very different from *sticks* when it comes to lighting a fire.

Dry sticks are seldom found on the ground,

they are best got from a tree. Find a tree with a dead branch or two, break these off, and you will have dry sticks. For "kindling," a number of sticks partly split or splintered with your knife are useful.

Do you know what "punk" is? Well, "punk," or "tinder," is what many backwoodsmen carry about with them for lighting their fires. It can be a small bit of cotton soaked in gas or alcohol, or very dry, baked fungus, or bark fibre, or anything that will catch fire from the slightest spark. **For a cooking fire, use plenty of sticks at first, as they make the hot ashes and embers which are most necessary for cooking.**

The Wilderness Expert says:

There are many ways to start a fire. You can even start one by rubbing wood against wood, using a small bow. But that takes a lot of practice. The easiest and quickest way to light one is with a small Bic lighter. Of course, you will need a parent's permission to carry one of those in your backpack.

How To Make A Shelter

"Let the boy remember also that in addition to courage, unselfishness, and fair dealing, he must have efficiency, he must have knowledge, he must cultivate a sound body and a good mind, and train himself so that he can act with quick decision in any crisis that may arise. Mind, eye, muscle, all must be trained so that the boy can master himself, and thereby learn to master his fate."

Theodore Roosevelt

THE LEAN-TO

In building your "lean-to," look for a couple of good trees standing from eight to ten feet apart with branches from six to eight feet above the ground. By studying the illustration below, you will be able to build a very serviceable shack, affording protection from the dews and rain How to "thatch" the lean- to is shown in the illustrations.

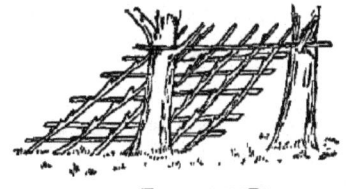

Frame of Lean To.

Method of Thatching.

After you have built your frame, you can gather branches (with the leaves still on) and hang them on the outside to make a perfect covering that will keep out rain and wind. Be sure to start from the bottom and work up, so that the layers overlap the top of the layer underneath. That way, the shelter will not leak.

If you find yourself in a heavy rain, it is also good to dig a small trench along the bottom to divert water off to the sides rather than into your shelter area.

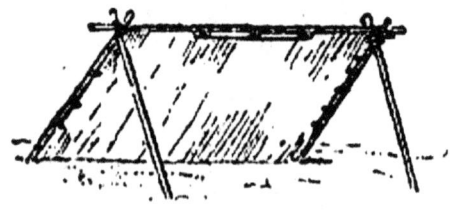

A BIVOUAC SHELTER.

NOTE: If pitched with its back to the wind, with a good fire in front, it can be made a most luxurious bedroom on cold night. The roof catches all the warmth and glow of the fire, The same type of structure can be built in a place without trees by using walking sticks, drift wood, or rope, and a six-foot tarp (or blanket).

If the camp site is to be used for several days,

two "lean-tos" may be built facing each other, about six feet apart. This will make a very comfortable camp, as a small fire can be built between the two, thus giving warmth and light.

THE TENT

This is a simple tent. The roof, or "fly," can be 6 ft. by 6 ft. Two poles, 3 ft. 6 in., should be planted firmly – at least six inches in the ground.

A stout ridge-rope should be stretched tightly between them, and tied at the top of each, and then securely fixed to a tent peg well driven into the ground in front of each end of the tent.

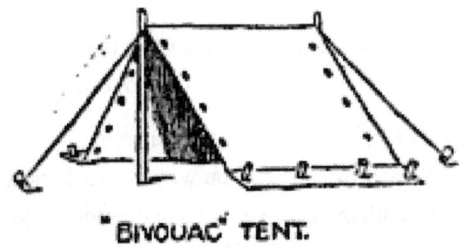

"BIVOUAC" TENT.

Other Variations

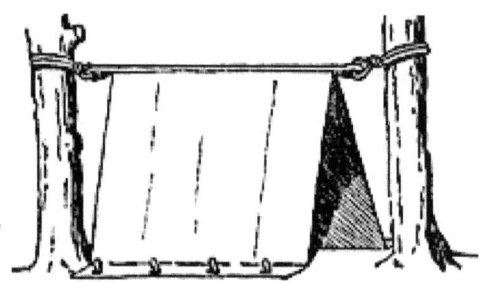

TREES INSTEAD OF TENT POLES.

HOW TO SLEEP IN COMFORT OUTDOORS:

The most important thing is remember that to keep warm and dry you want more thickness underneath than above you. On the floor of your "lean-to" lay a thick layer of the "fans" or branches of trees with the leaves still on, with the ends of the stems toward the foot of the bed. Now thatch this over with more "fans" by thrusting the ends through the first layer at a slight angle toward the head of the bed, so that the soft tips will curve toward the foot of the bed.

Be sure to make the head of your bed away from the opening of the "lean-to" and the foot toward the opening. Over this bed spread your blanket or sleeping bag. If you don't have anything for cover, you can use leafy branches over the top of you, as well. You will be surprised how soft, springy, and fragrant a bed like this can be.

You can also make a comfortable bed by tying two ends of a blanket with rope and tying them to the trunks of two trees. This makes a comfortable hammock if you would rather not sleep on the groud.

Bough Bed

Sir Robert's Tent Hammock

"I have made a sketch of my tent, which, as you will see, is a kind of hammock with a roof to it, slung between two trees. This form of tent keeps you dry in wet weather or on swampy ground; you never have to lie on the ground; you can't get snakes and other nice visitors crawling into your bed. The hammock is long enough to hold your kit as well as yourself.

It is kept stretched out by two side poles and a ridge pole. These can be cut in the wood where you camp, and the hammock itself, with bedding and kit inside, can be rolled up in the tarp for packing.

The hammock is springy and most comfortable to sleep in. When you are ill or wounded it makes a very good stretcher, the side poles forming the carrying handles. In the same way, when you are dead it makes an excellent coffin, as the sides and ends fold in, and can be laced over the body. I have not tried it myself in that way.

Another advantage which I have twice found the cot-tent to have was, when a tornado visited camp, and all the tents were blown down into the mud, my little cot was swaying quietly in the wind – it cannot blow down."

Tent Hammock

THE SLEEPING BAG COVER

An even simpler form of comfort in the outdoors is a tarp about three feet longer than a sleeping bag, folded and sewn into two compartments. The bottom is for stuffing with leaves or boughs with leaves still on, and your sleeping bag goes in the top layer.

The object of having long flaps is seen in the illustration. The lower one can be rolled with your spare clothes inside it to form your pillow, while the upper one can be supported by a crossbar to form a little roof over your head. In a sleeping bag of this kind, if waterproof, you can sleep out without a tent at all.

Sleeping Bag Cover

NOTE: You can find a more detailed description of how to set up a comfortable campsite--as well as many tricks and tips for surviving outdoors in *Scouting For Boys*, which was written by Robert Baden-Powell in 1908. It is available for free at many places online.

What To Do If You Are Lost

"If you are troubled or anxious, or in pain, force yourself to smile. It will be difficult at first; still, force yourself to do it, and you will find to your surprise that your trouble is not so great as you thought it was.

I have known men in action getting very anxious when great danger overshadowed them. But if one began to talk cheerily, or to whistle, the cloud passed by and everybody bucked up and was ready to face the situation."

—Sir Robert Baden-Powell

S — STOP

If you think you might have gone off course, stop. It's tempting to "keep going just a little further," but you'll often get even more tangled if you keep going.

T — THINK

Put the feeling of panic aside. Stay calm, and try to approach the situation rationally. Consider what made you realize you were lost—a com-pass read-ing, a trail that sud-denly dis-ap-peared, or the absence of a landmark that you are supposed to see. Stay put while you think, and assess the situation—moving is more likely to make things worse.

O — OBSERVE

Check out your surroundings and consider what landmarks might help you situate yourself. Compare your observations to your map, which could help you get reoriented. Consider how the weather looks, what time of day it is, and what supplies you have on hand. All of these factors will help you develop an action plan.

P — PLAN

Brainstorm potential next steps and decide on a plan. You might choose to camp out overnight, wait-ing for day-light to make your next move. If you feel confident that you can get back on track, leave a trail marking the path you take (like a breadcrumb trail, but use rocks or some other marker).

The Wilderness Expert says: There are times when the best plan is to wait for help. If you decide to do this, you can help rescuers find you by spelling the word help, or SOS on the ground using rocks and sticks. Or make a large arrow with them pointing to where you are. Do anything you can think of to attract attention.

Finding Your Way

A good habit to get into when you are hiking or camping in wilderness places, is to **make a note of your surroundings before you leave**. Here are some questions to ask yourself that will help you do that.

WHERE IS NORTH FROM HERE?
(If you note what direction you are traveling in when you leave, you will then have a good idea of which direction to walk in order to get back there)

ARE THERE ANY LANDMARKS AROUND YOU?
(Such as a particularly tall tree, or a certain view of a nearby mountain, or maybe even a road close by)

DO YOU HAVE A MAP TO FOLLOW?
(If not, try making one of your own as you go along, then you will be able to follow it back to where you started from)

DID YOU LET SOMEONE KNOW YOUR INTENTIONS AND WHERE YOU WOULD BE BEFORE YOU STARTED OUT?
(This will help others know where to look for you if you don't come back in a reasonable amount of time)

YOU CAN ALSO BLAZE A TRAIL AS YOU GO
(Do this by leaving small signs that you will recognize on your way back, such as a pile of rocks in an obvious area, a broken twig along the trail, or even an arrow scratched in the dirt, pointing in the direction you are walking.)

The Wilderness Expert says: The more you practice being aware of your surroundings at all times, the less likely you are to get lost when you are out and about. Keeping a compass and pocket notebook on hand can help a lot, too. It's good to carry your own backup!

How To Find North

THE COMPASS

The **needle on a compass** always points to the North. Turn until you are facing the same way the needle is pointing. This is north.

THE SHADOW METHOD

You can use the **Shadow Method** if you have enough direct sunlight to get a shadow. Put a medium size stick into the ground and place a rock at the end of the shadow it makes. Wait fifteen minutes. Place another rock at the end of where the shadow has moved to. Put your left toe on the first rock. Put your right toe on the second rock. Now you are facing north.

THE SUN

The Sun always rises (before noon) in the East, and sets (after noon) in the West. Face the sun. Hold both arms straight out from your sides. In the morning, North will be on your left. In the afternoon, it will be on your right. At noon the sun is straight overhead, so it will have to be at least an hour before or after so that you can tell which direction the sun is moving.

It's always a good idea to find which direction North is, and make a note of it, whenever you enter a wilderness area. You should also note any distinguishing landmarks (a particular tree, rock formation, gate, etc.) that are there, too. Knowing this will help you get back if you get turned around or lost when you are exploring.

AT NIGHT

The northern sky is a large clock, with Polaris (the **North Star**) at its center. The hour hand is a line drawn through *Dubhe* and *Merak*, the two pointer stars of the Big Dipper. Because the stars make a full circle around the North Star in 23 hours 56 minutes, you can learn to read it well with a little practice.

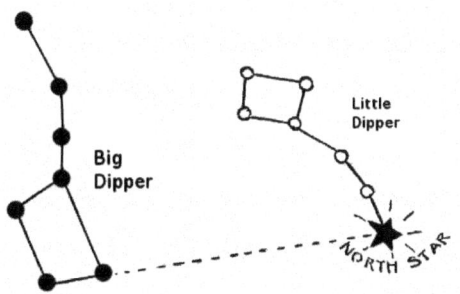

Some Good Things To Know

If your head gets too hot put green leaves inside of your hat. If your throat is parched, and you cannot get water, put a pebble in your mouth. This will start the saliva and quench the thirst.

Indians had a way of purifying water from a pond or swamp by digging a hole about one foot across and down about six inches below the water level, a few feet from the pond. After it had filled with water, they bailed it out quickly, repeating the bailing process about three times. After the third bailing the hole would fill with filtered water.

Boiling water for 5-20 minutes is the best and safest way to kill germs.

Surrounding the campfire with rocks is a great way of prolonging the heat from the fire. The rocks will stay warm long after the flames have extinguished. Small hot stones can also be used to boil water.

All you need to do is to drop a few hot rocks in your metal water container. The heat from the rocks is enough to bring the water to a boil, making it safe to drink.

An **SOS** signal is the universal call for help. You can use light as well as sound to give the signal. The message is: **three dots followed by three dashes followed by three dots.** If you're using light, an SOS signal would be three short bursts of light, followed by three long bursts, followed by three more short bursts. The same applies if you are using sound. You can signal with a flashlight, whistle, mirror, etc.

COURAGE

"If you are troubled or anxious, or in pain, force yourself to smile. It will be difficult at first; still, force yourself to do it, than you will find to your surprise that your trouble is not so great as you thought it was.

I have known men in action getting very anxious when great danger overshadowed them. But if one began to laugh and to talk cheerily, or to whistle, the cloud passed by and everybody bucked up and was ready to face the situation."

Sir Robert Baden-Powell

"Growing up is thinking for yourself."

A Prayer If You Are In Serious Trouble
(Really)

The Lord is my shepherd; I shall not want.
He makes me lie down in green pastures.
He leads me beside still waters.
He restores my soul.
He leads me in paths of righteousness
for his name's sake.
Even though I walk through the valley of
the shadow of death, I will fear no evil,
for you are with me;
your rod and your staff, they comfort me.
You prepare a table before me in the
presence of my enemies; you anoint my
head with oil; my cup overflows.
Surely goodness and mercy shall follow me
all the days of my life, and I shall dwell in the
house of the Lord forever.

◆——————▶

The Wilderness Expert says: He hasn't gone through any serious trouble that didn't get better after he prayed about it. A good thing to know in case you ever find yourself in one of those situations. Because it could happen to anybody.

About Sir Robert

Sir Robert Baden-Powell is a real life hero, who wrote a book that boys all over the world learned the secrets of survival from. As the youngest colonel in the British Army, he was given an impossible job. To go into enemy territory and pretend he had a force of frontiersmen big enough to win the war. The odds were four to one... counting a cadet corps of boys from the ages of ten to sixteen.

He trained these boys to stand guard duty, run messages between patrols, and pick up the dead and wounded from off the battlefield. Some of them even acted as spies. This freed up the "real men" for actual fighting. In a siege that lasted 217 days, his small group finally won an amazing victory.

But he had a surprise waiting for him at home. The little manual he had written for "his boys" on how to survive, was being read by other boys everywhere. Boys who wanted to follow Sir Robert Baden-Powell. So many boys that the King of England finally said he could do more for his country by training all these boys rather than fighting in wars.

Which he did. It was a movement that spread around the world within his own lifetime. That was the beginning of the Boy Scouts.

Most of the information in this guide was taken from the writings of this brilliant outdoorsman.

About the Wilderness Expert

After a career in the Coast Guard, and many years working with youth programs, Jason Graham knows a lot about survival in the wilderness. He is also the author of The Ladybug Buddies Adventures, which had their beginnings as bedtime stories which he told to his own children. He enjoys hearing from readers, and you can get in touch with him by sending an email to:

Wilderness-Expert@SummersIslandPress.com

A Note to Readers...

Thank you for reading this book. If you enjoyed it, tell someone! If you would like to read other books like this, you can find them by visiting:

SummersIslandPress.com

You will also find the **Wilderness Kids Club** over there. It's a place to learn about Nature and meet other kids who also like to spend time in the "Great Outdoors." Our Wilderness Expert is on hand there, too, and can answer any questions you might have about the wilderness and how to explore the pieces nearest to you.

A Note to Parents...

Summers Island Press and Wilderness Kids Club are divisions of the Wilderness School Institute, a nonprofit educational organization based in Alaska. They are dedicated to giving children something better to do, and bringing more hope and heroes into their lives. For more information, or to find out how you can become involved in some of their exciting projects, please visit:

WildernessSchoolInstitute.org

www.ingramcontent.com/pod-product-compliance
Lightning Source LLC
Chambersburg PA
CBHW070804040426
42333CB00061B/2444